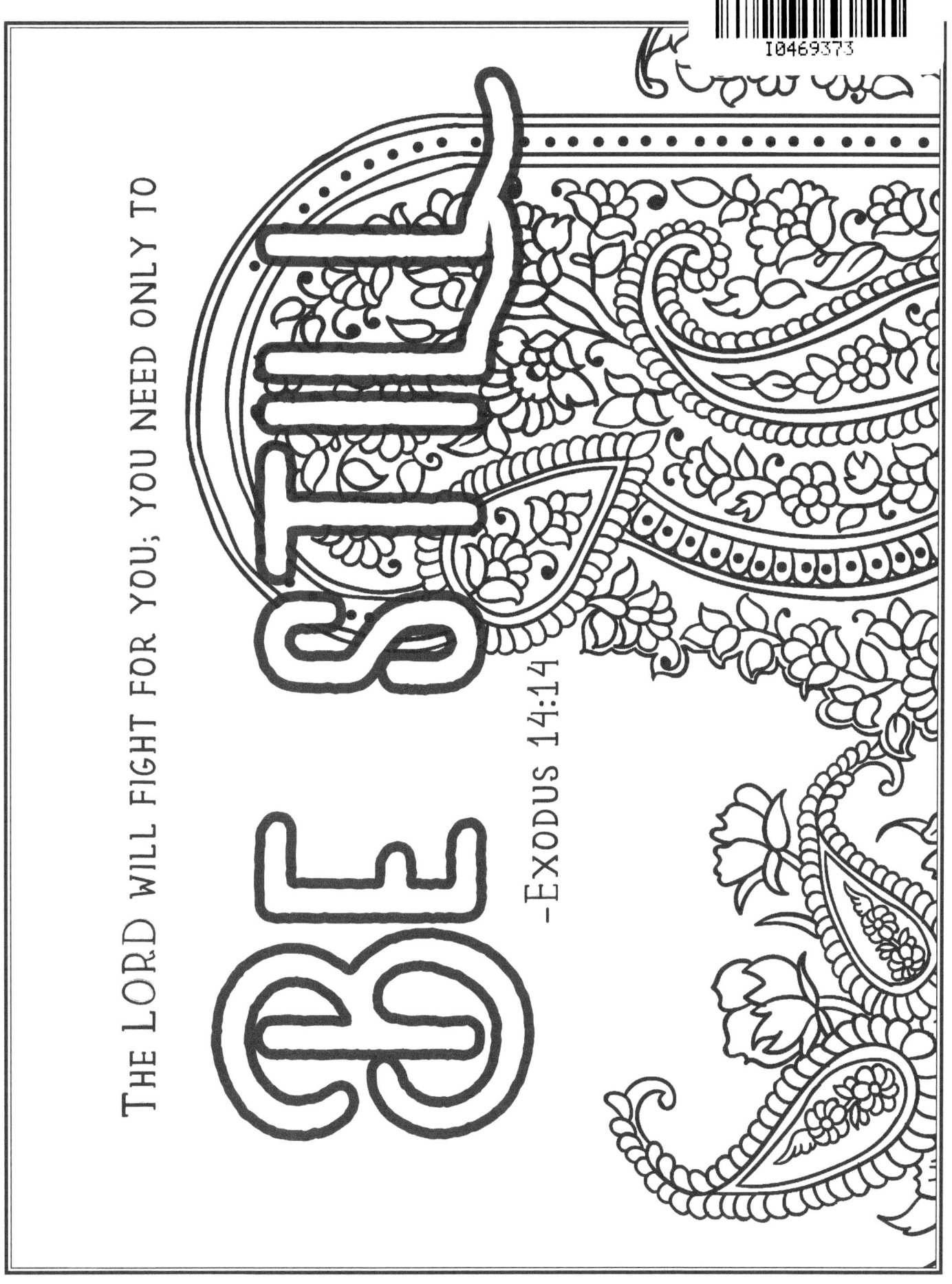

BE STILL

THE LORD WILL FIGHT FOR YOU; YOU NEED ONLY TO

—Exodus 14:14

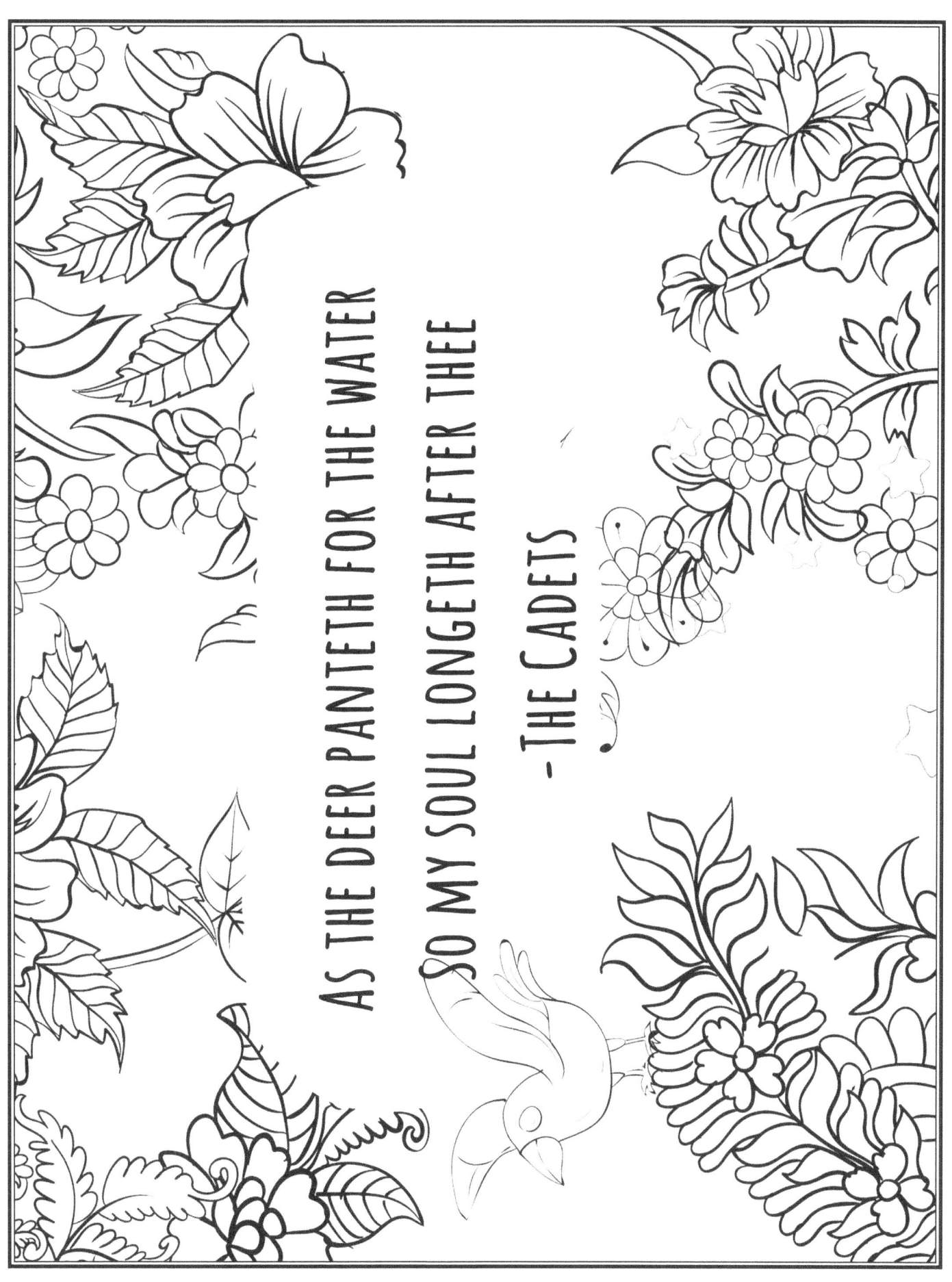

As the deer panteth for the water
So my soul longeth after thee
—The Cadets

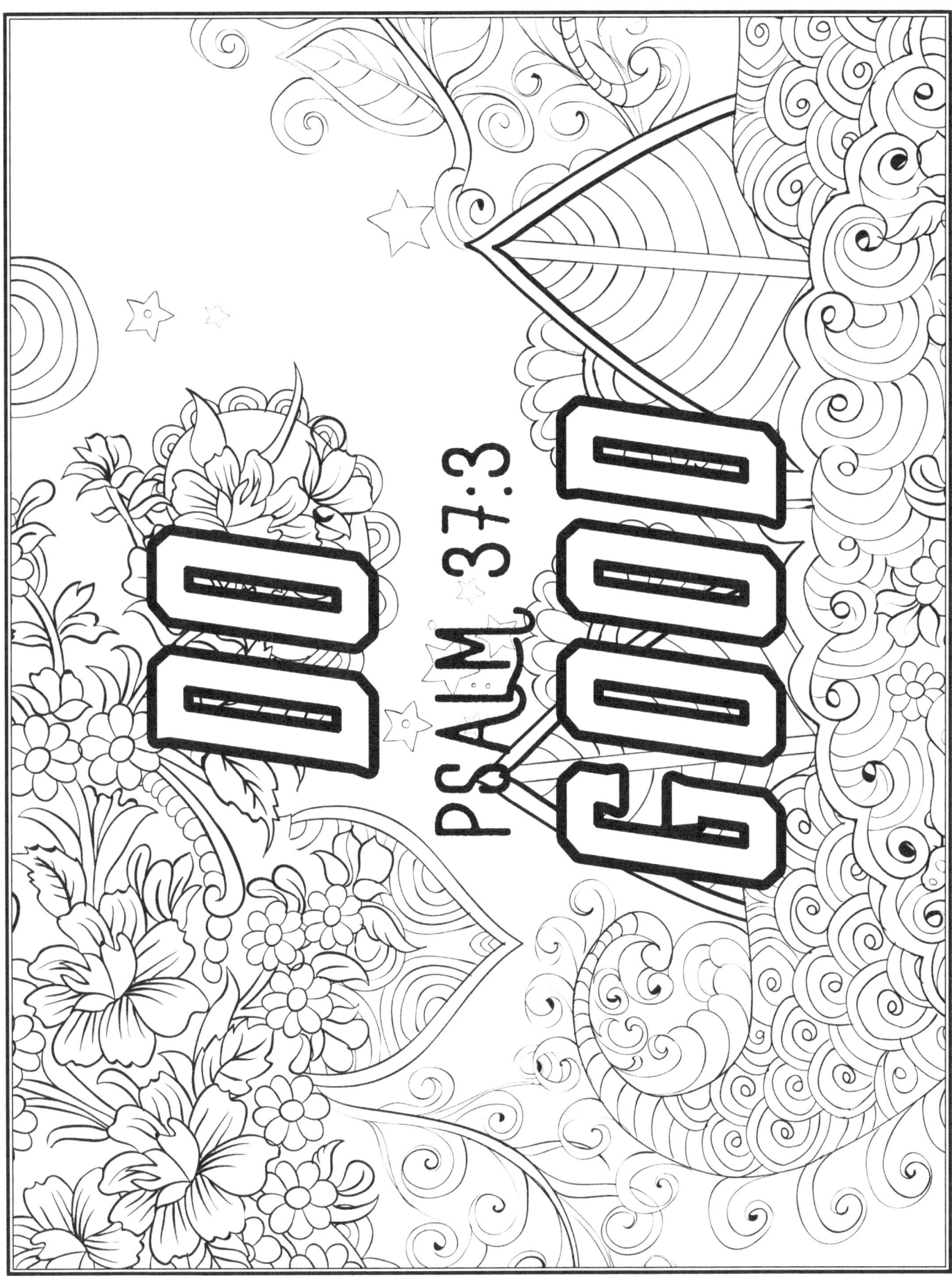

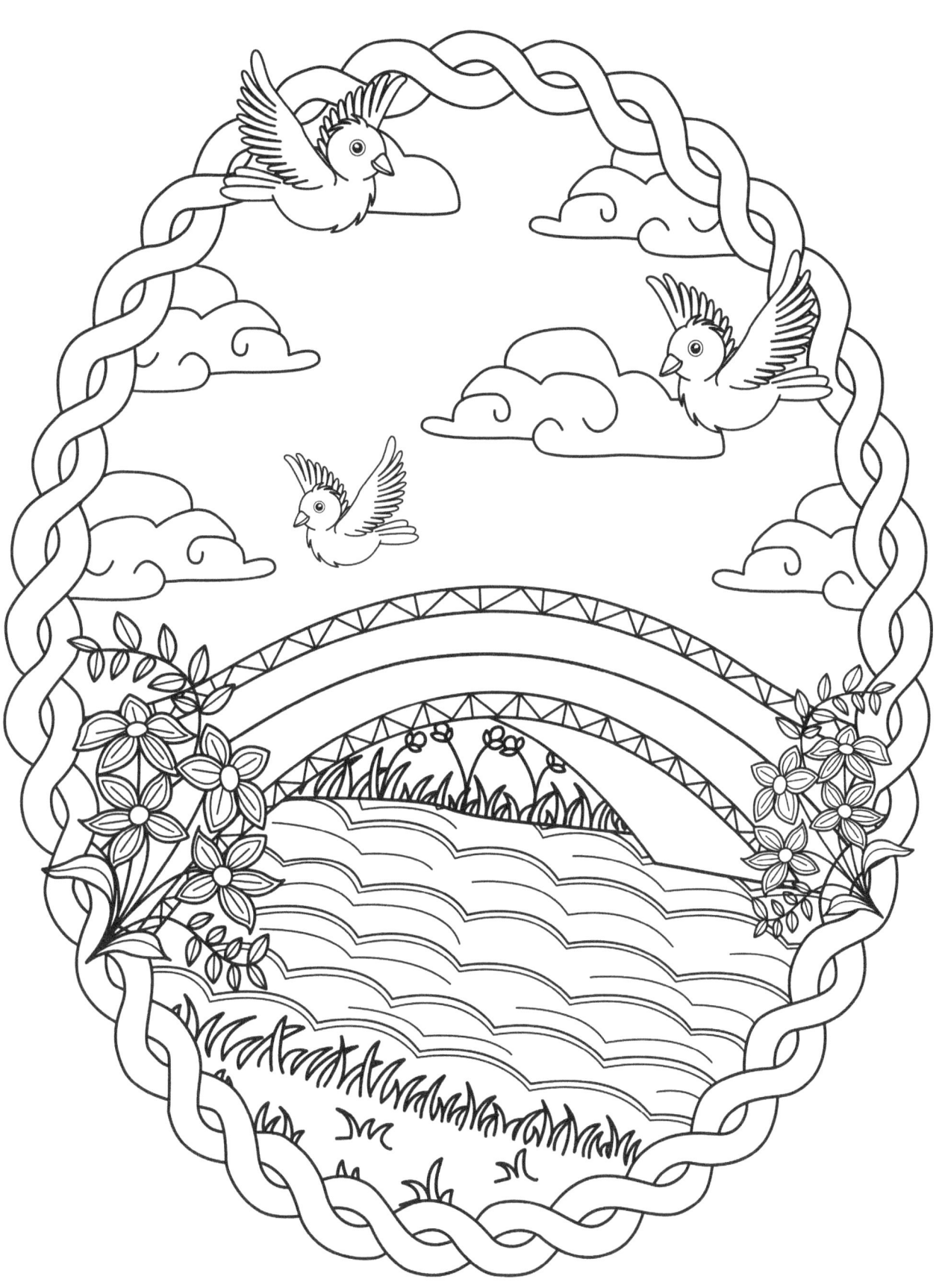

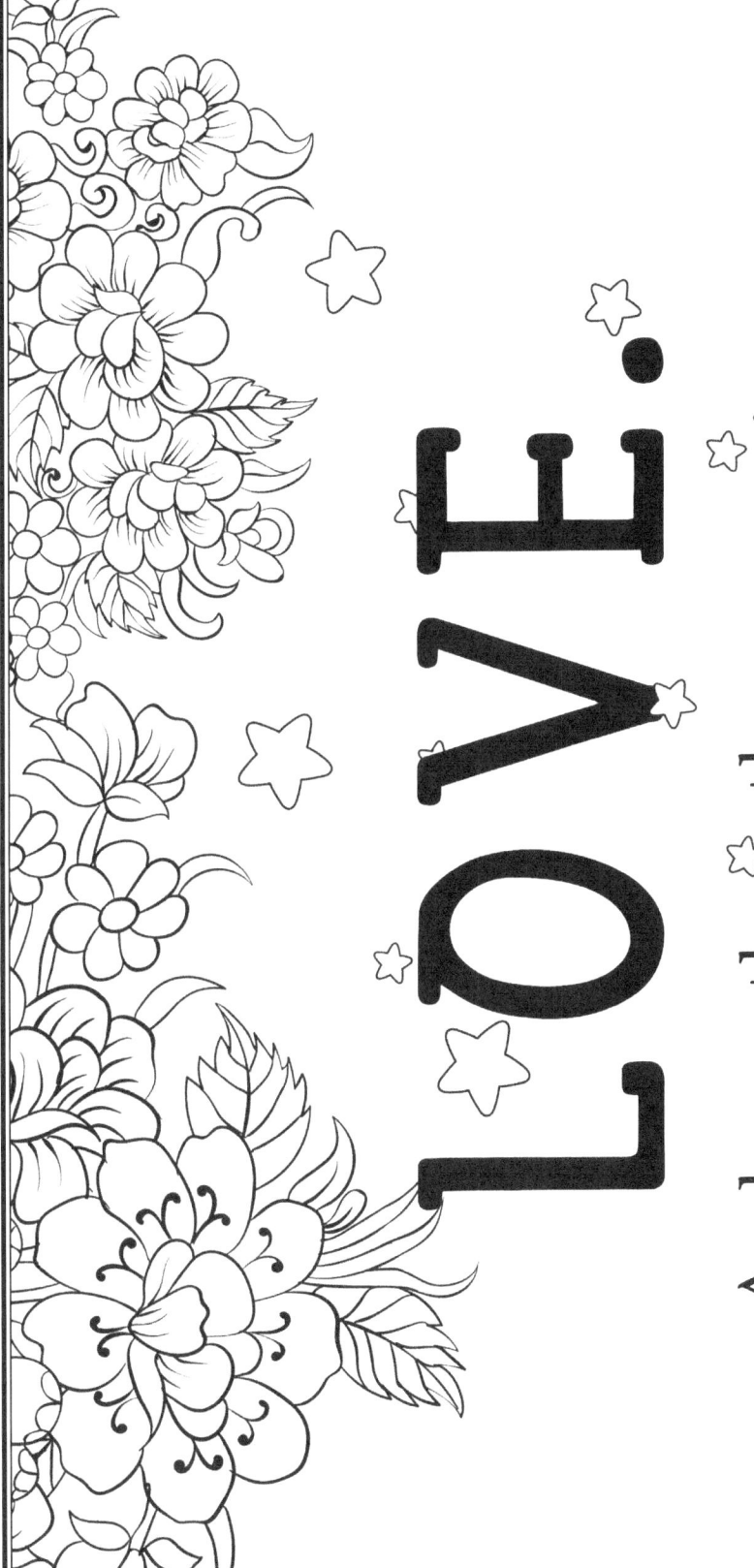

LOVE.

And now these three remain:

faith, hope and love.

But the greatest of these is love.

1 CORINTHIANS 13:13

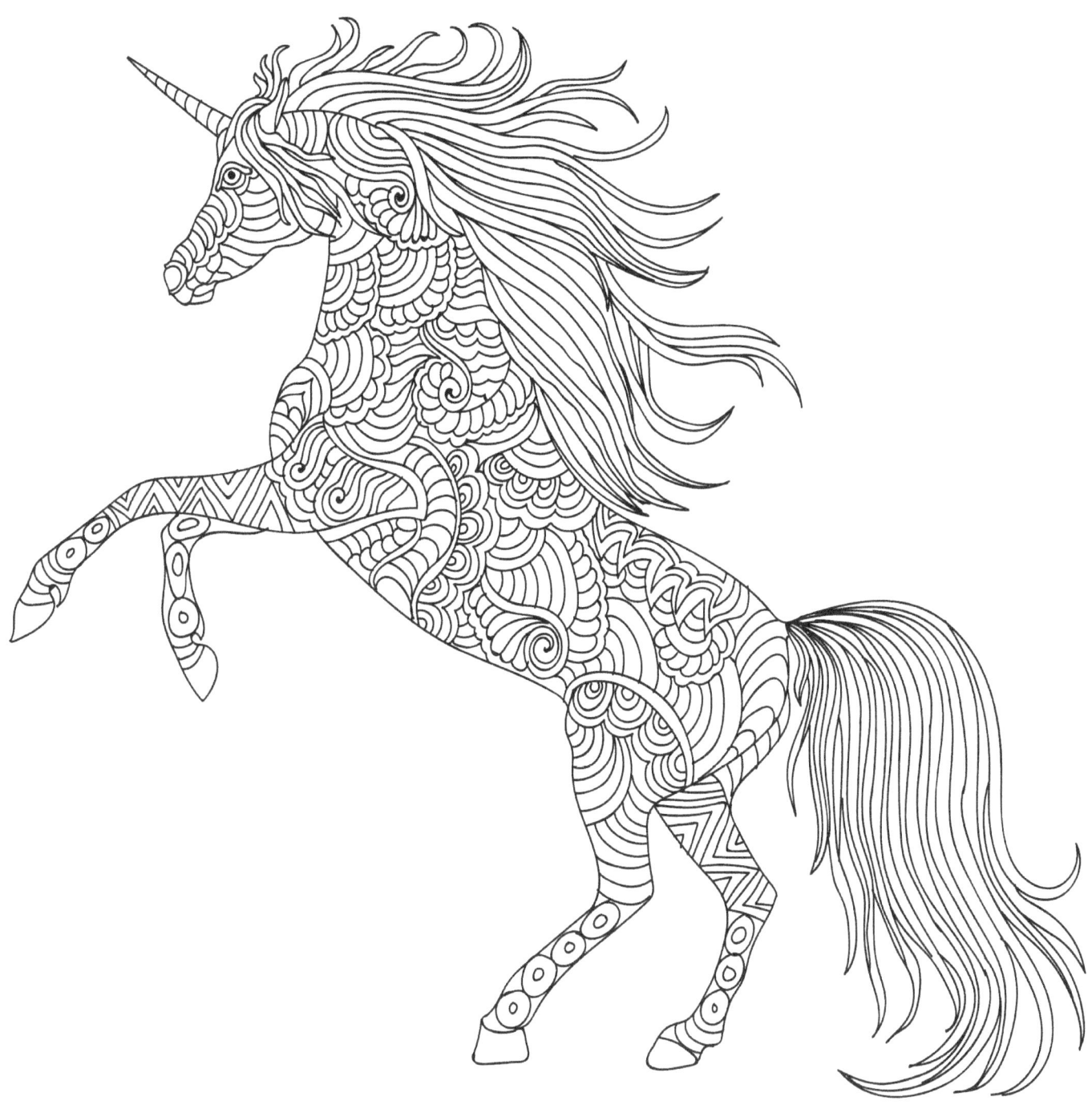

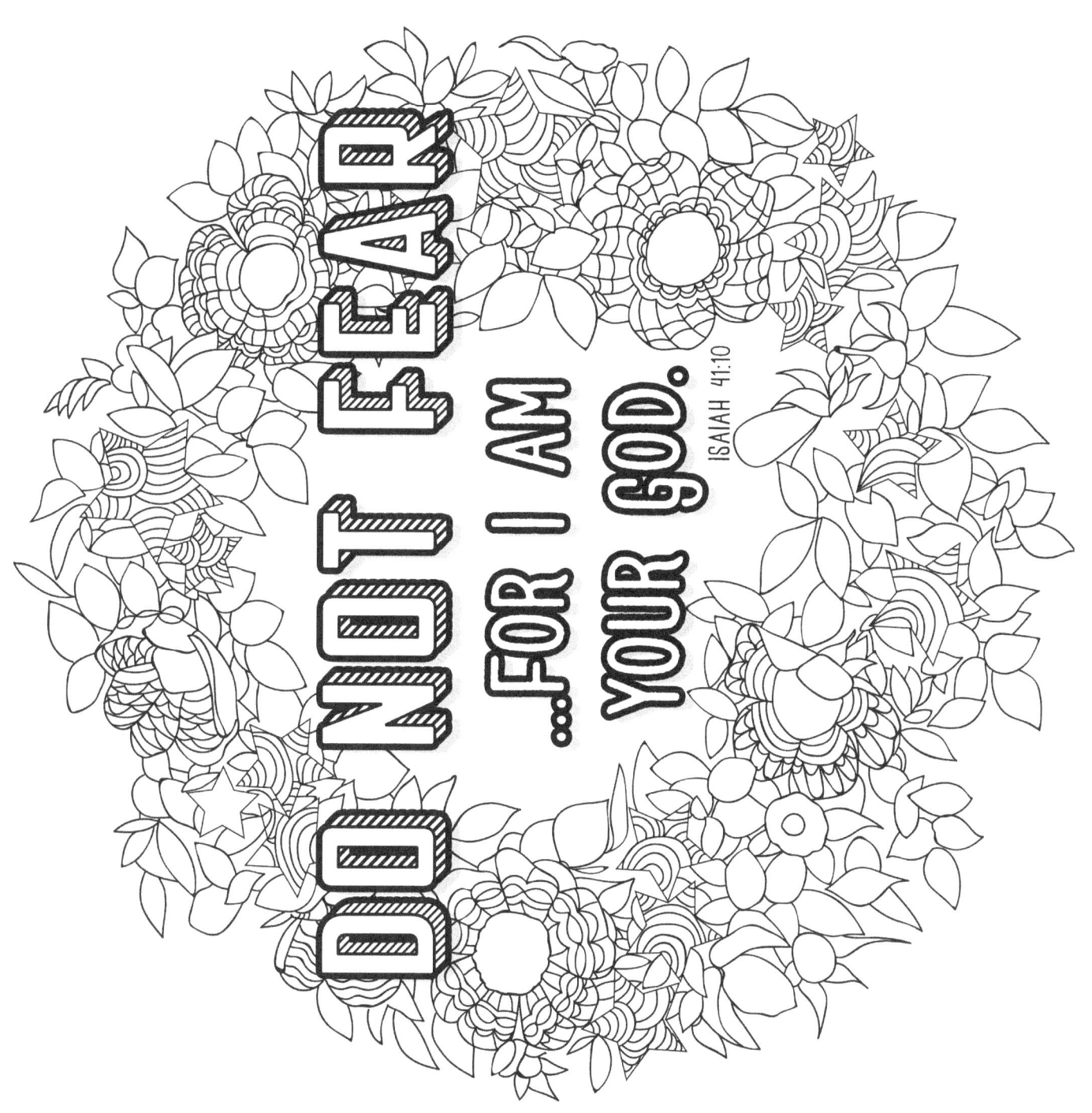

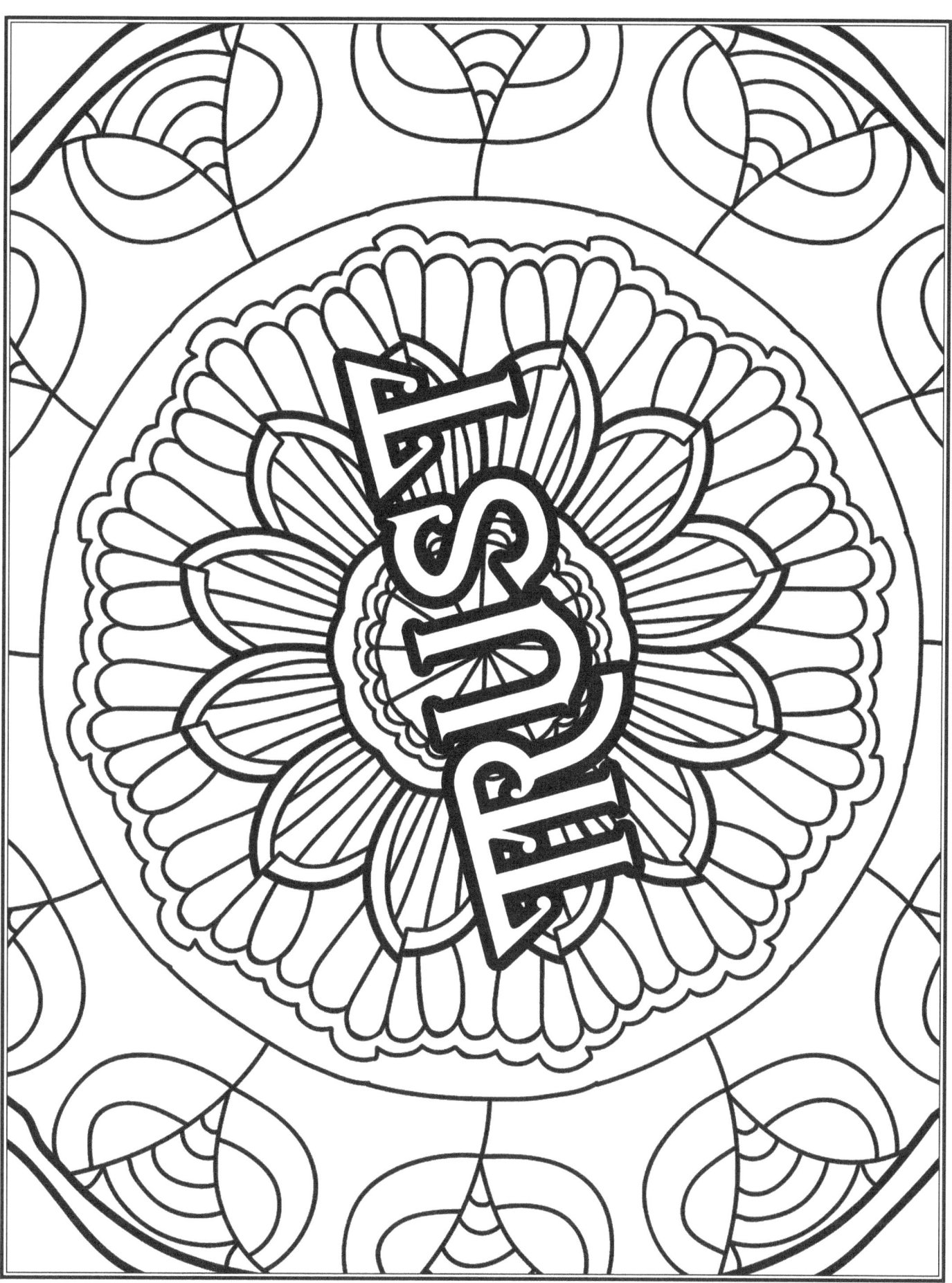

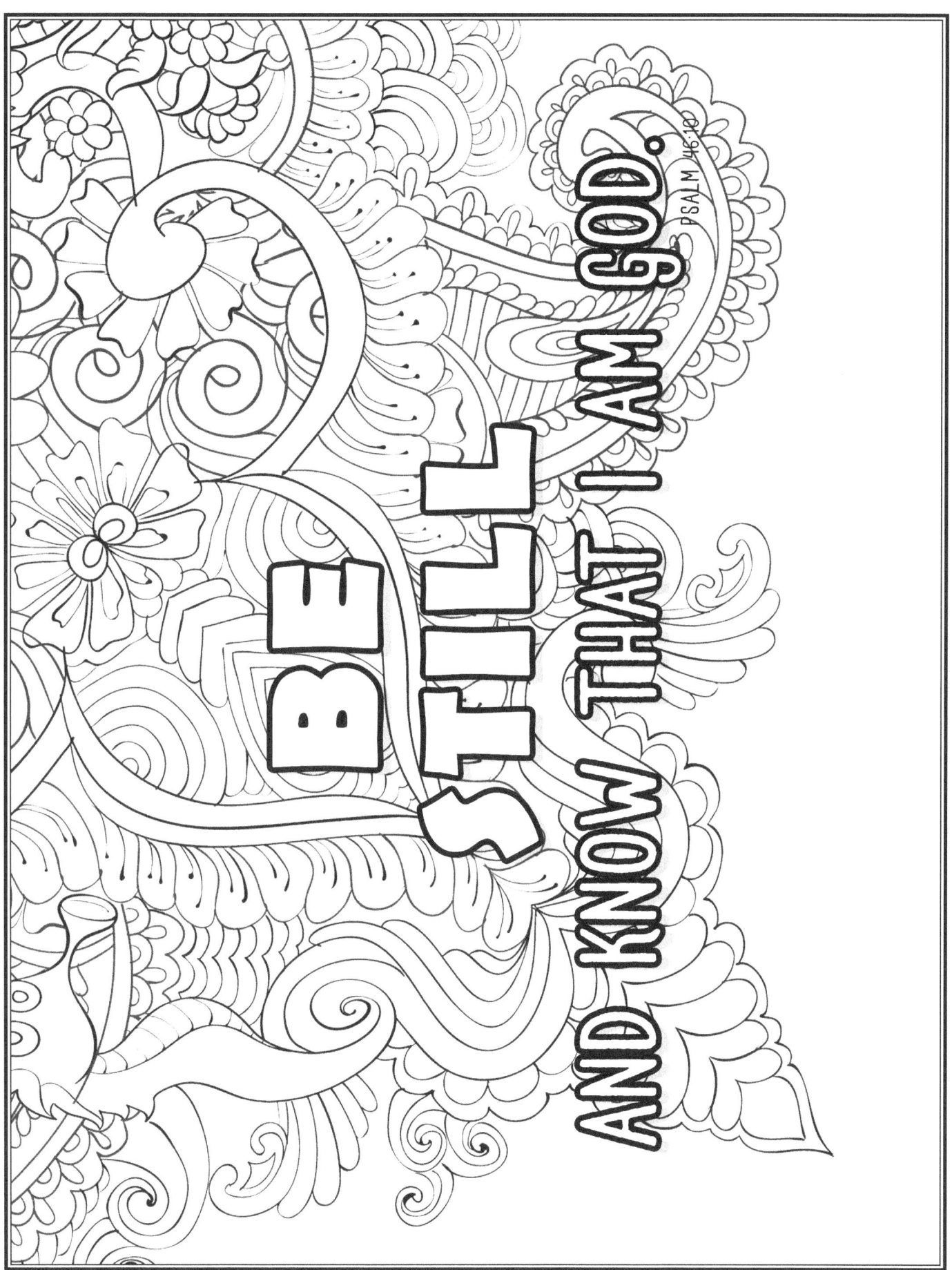

BE STILL AND KNOW THAT I AM GOD.

PSALM 46:10

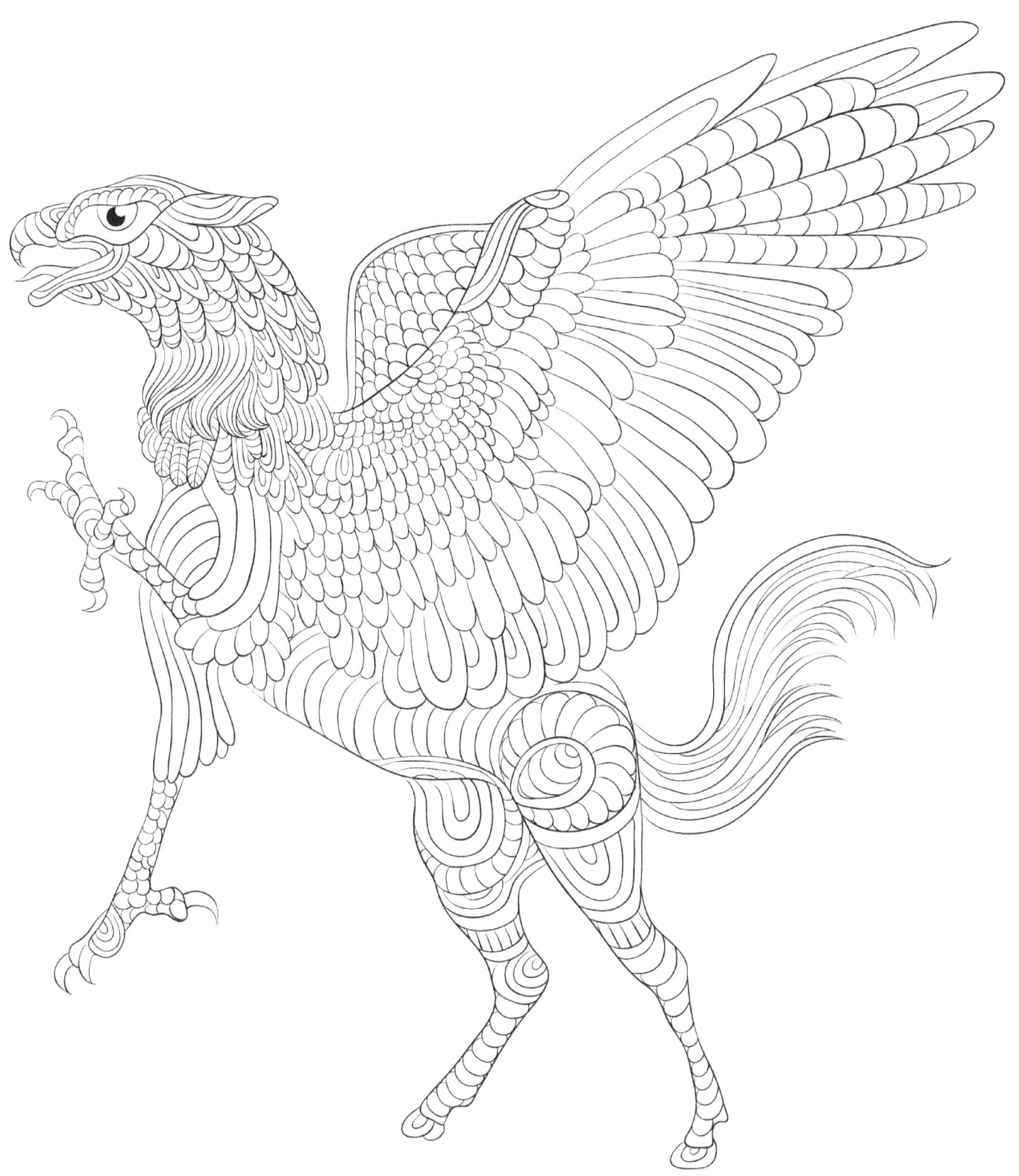

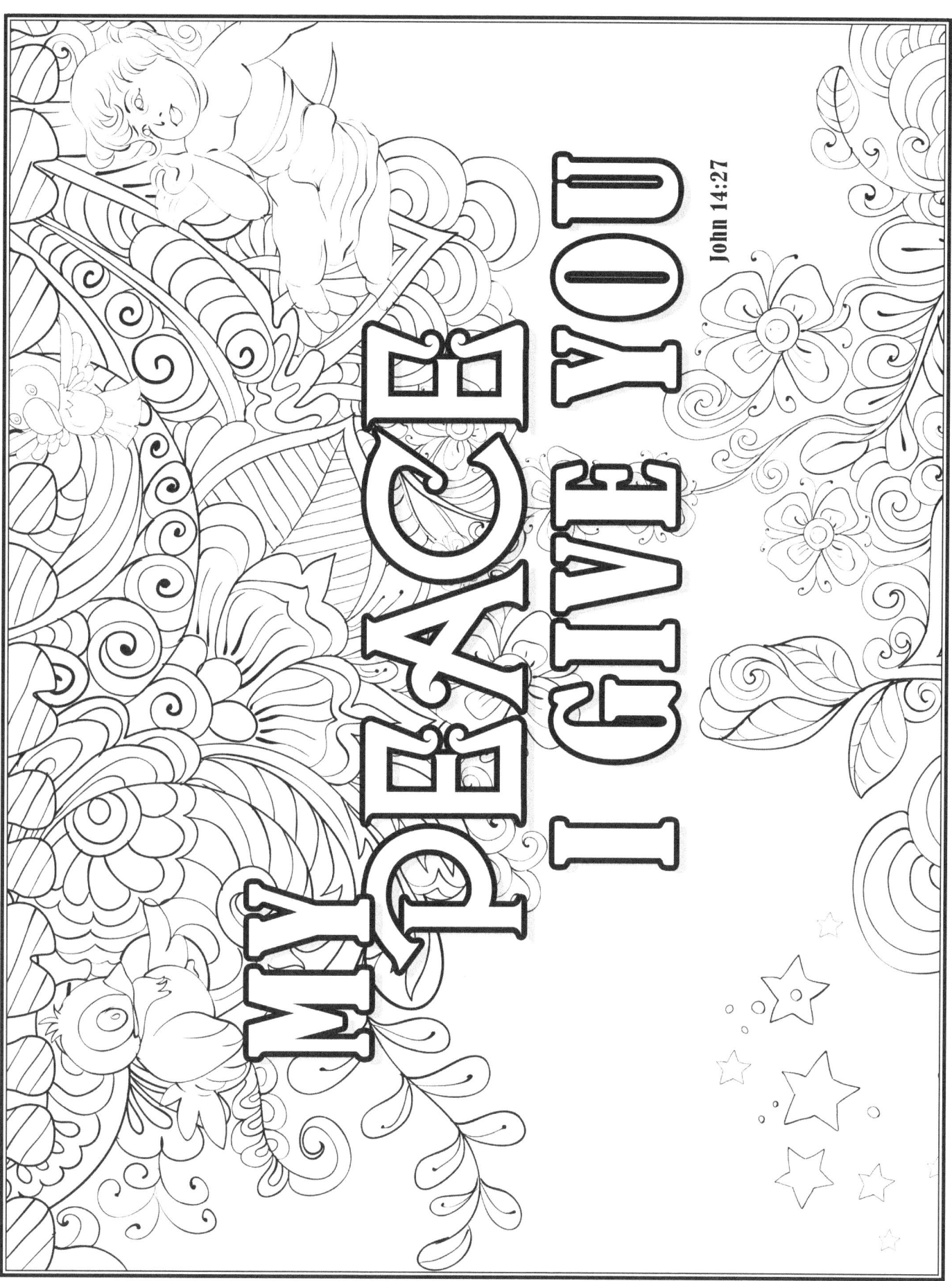

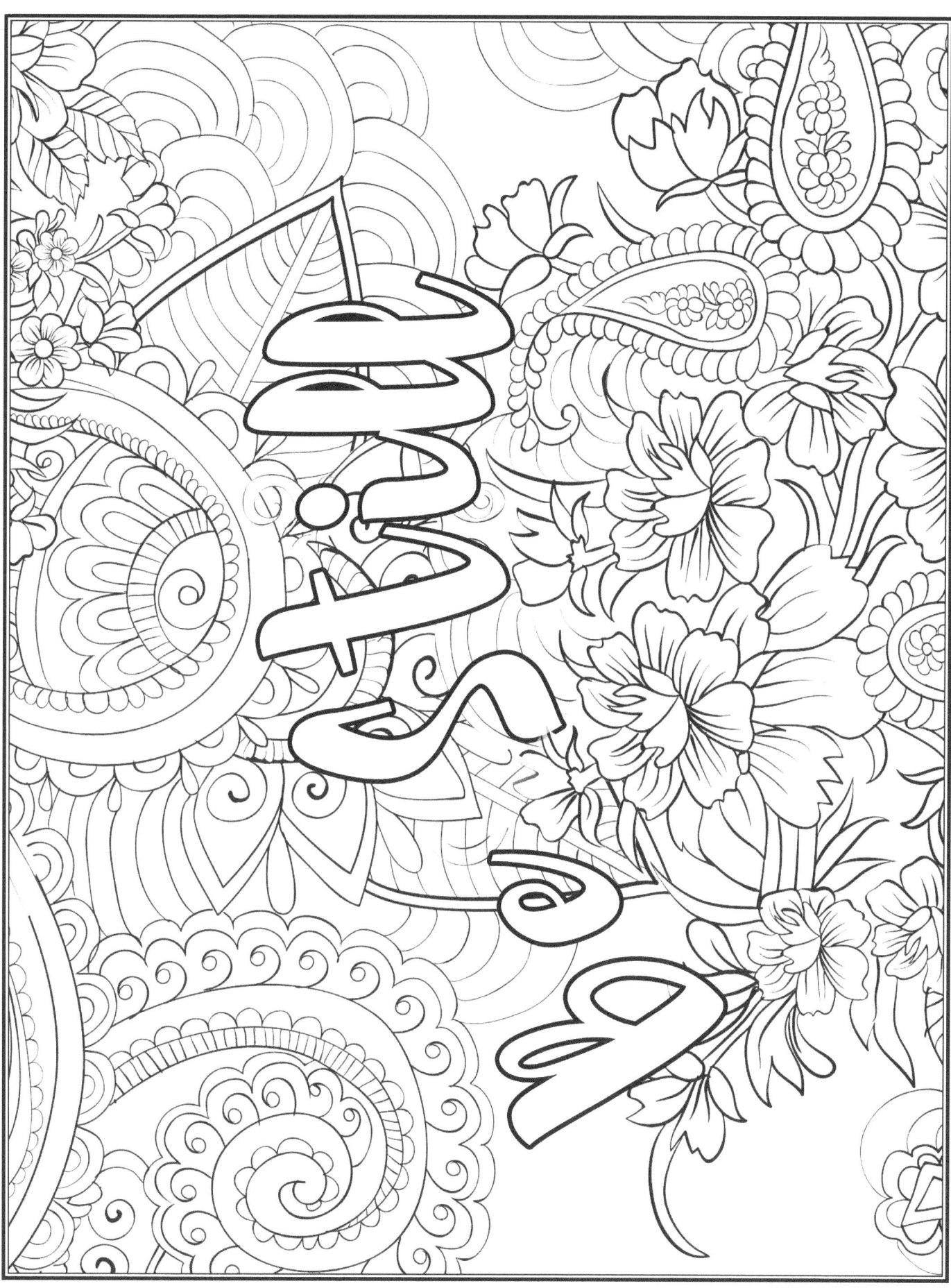

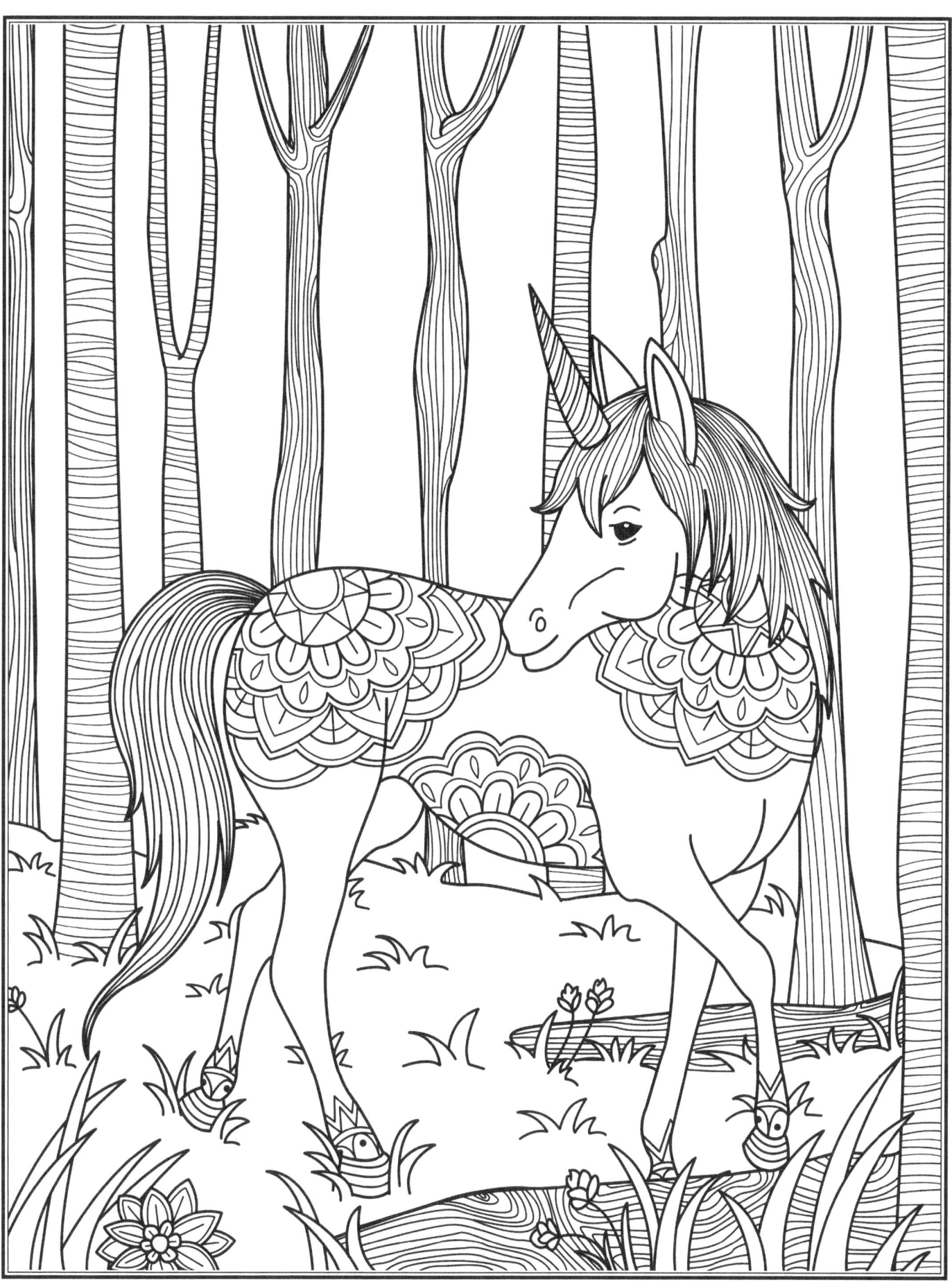

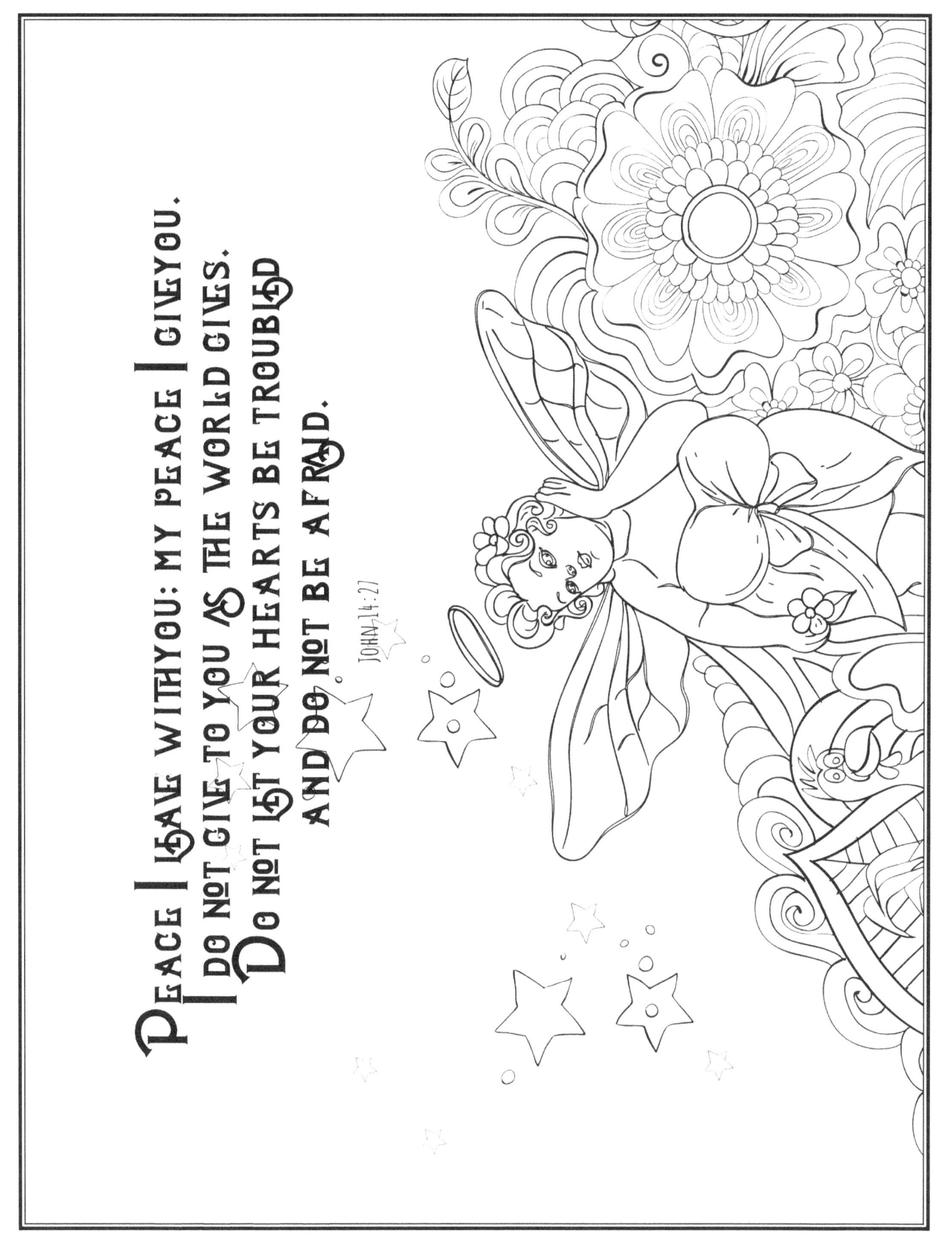

Peace I leave with you; my peace I give you. I do not give to you as the world gives. Do not let your hearts be troubled and do not be afraid.

John 14:27

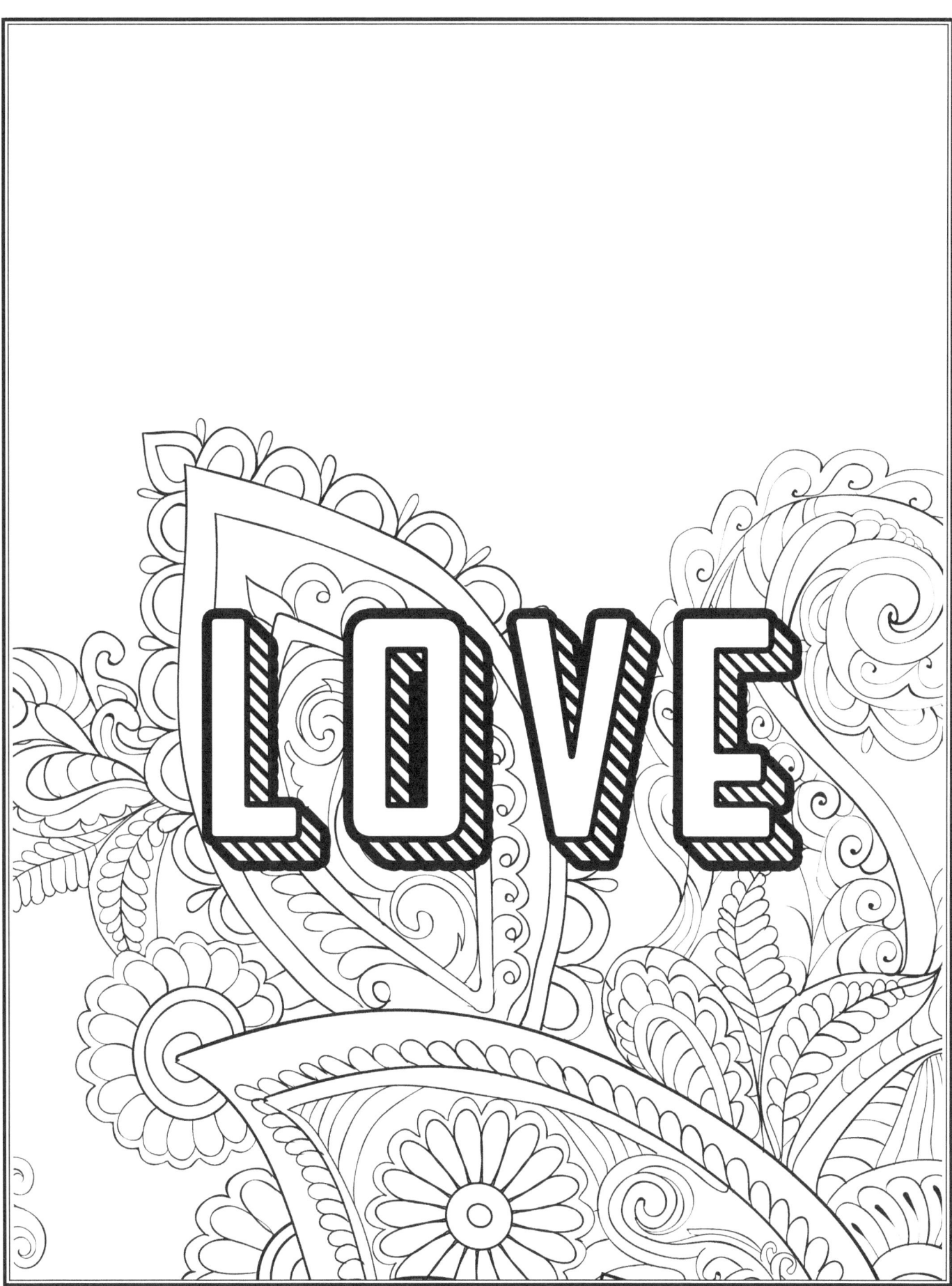

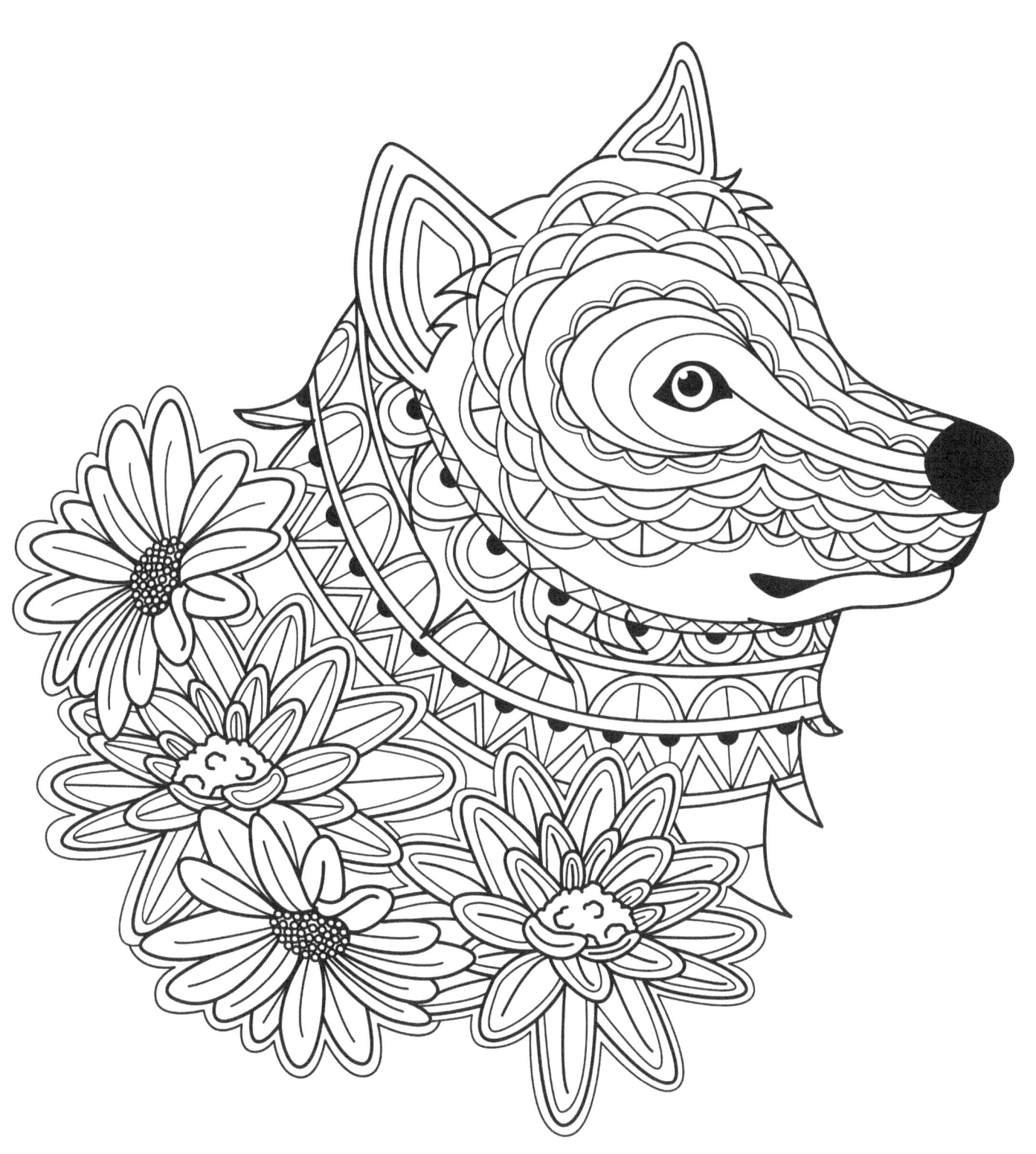

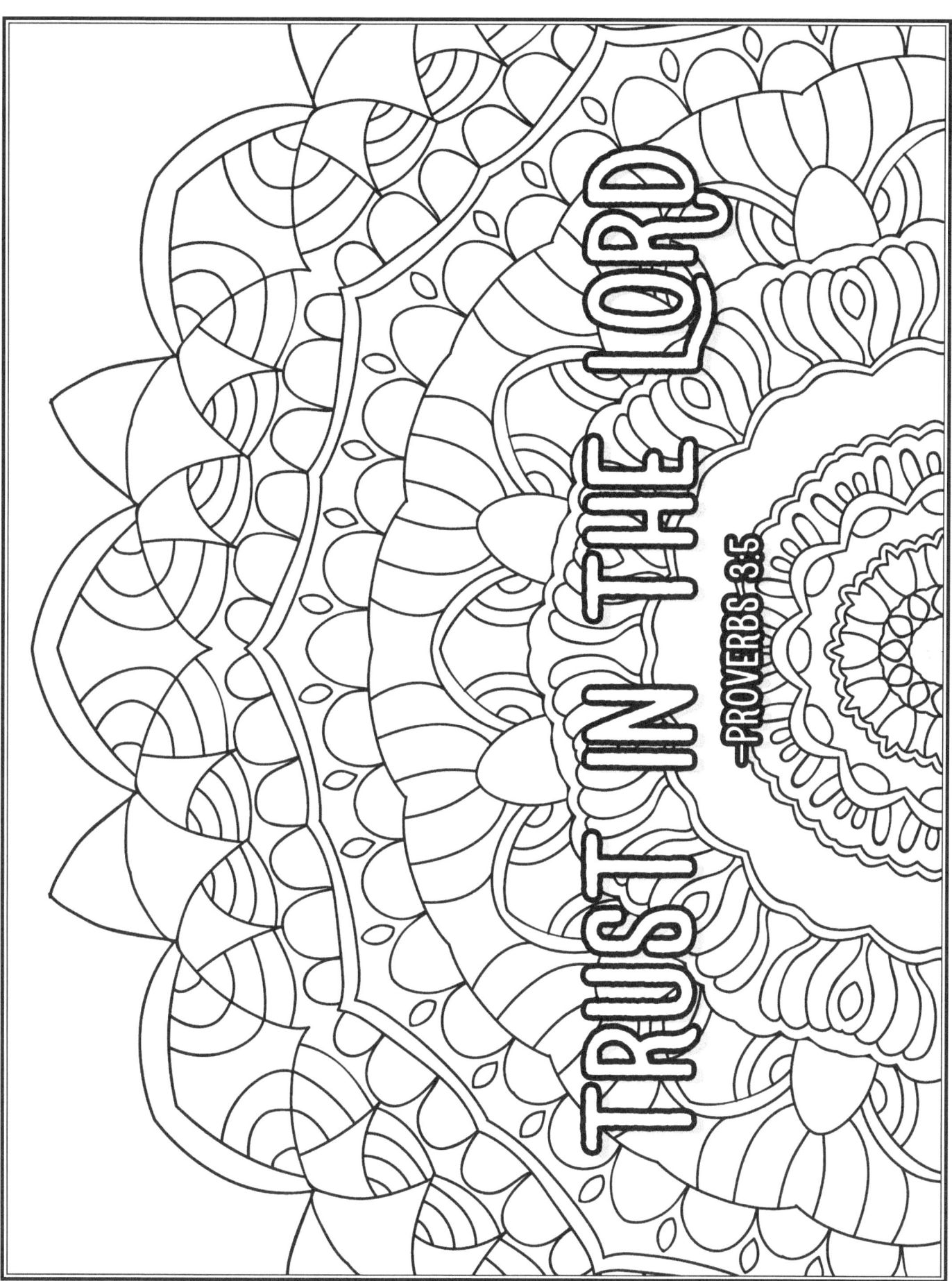

TRUST IN THE LORD

—PROVERBS 3:5

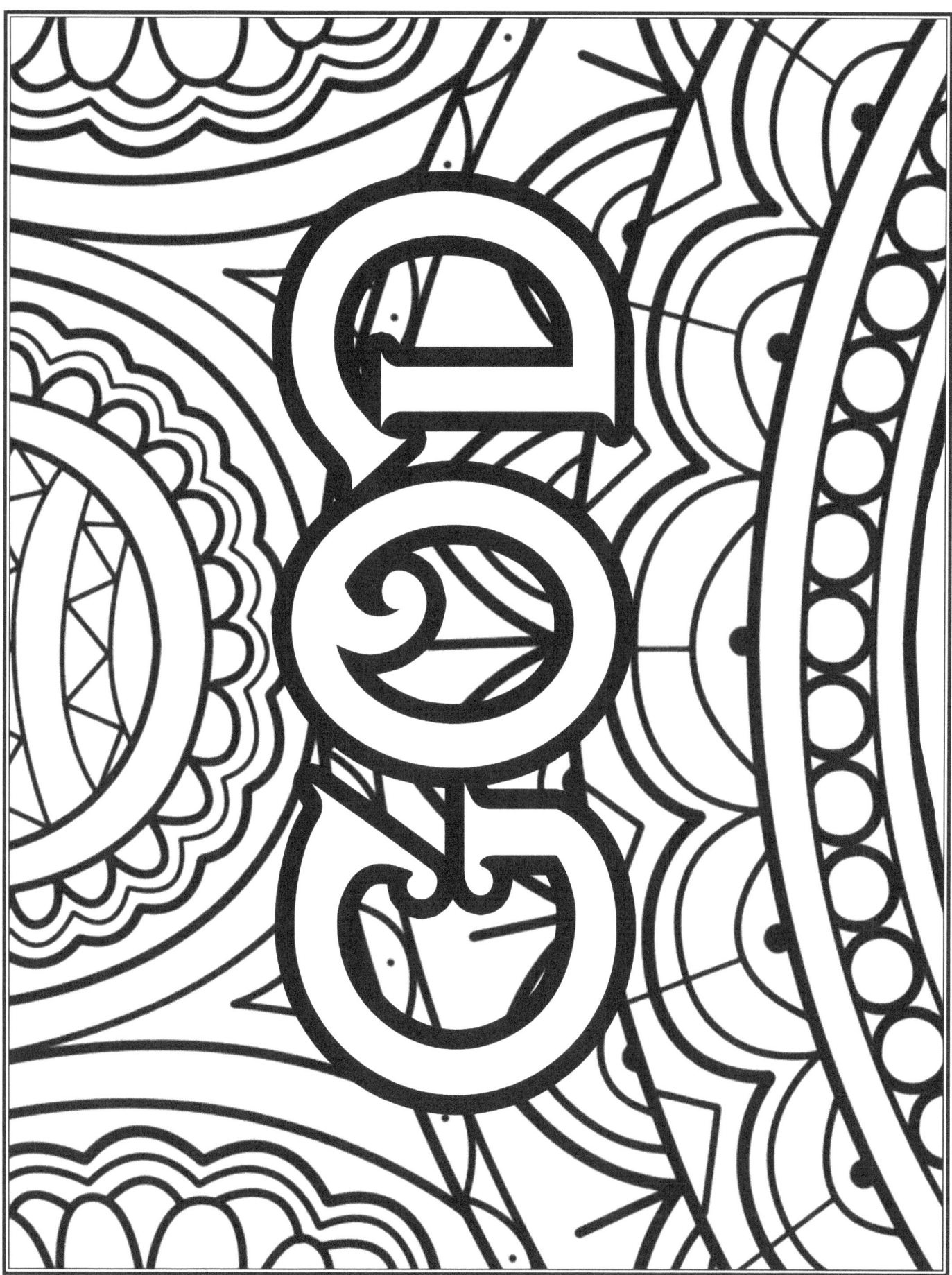

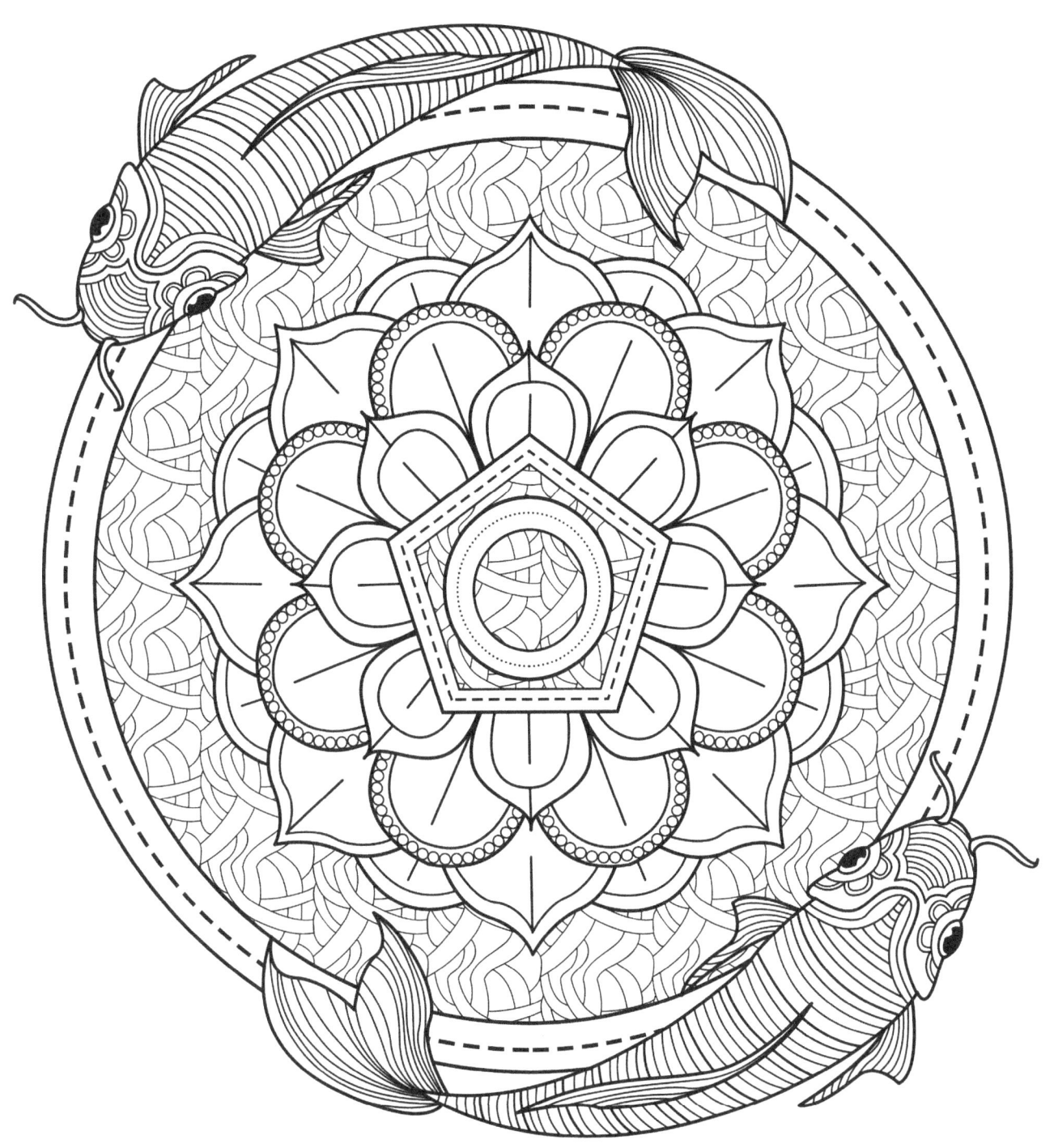

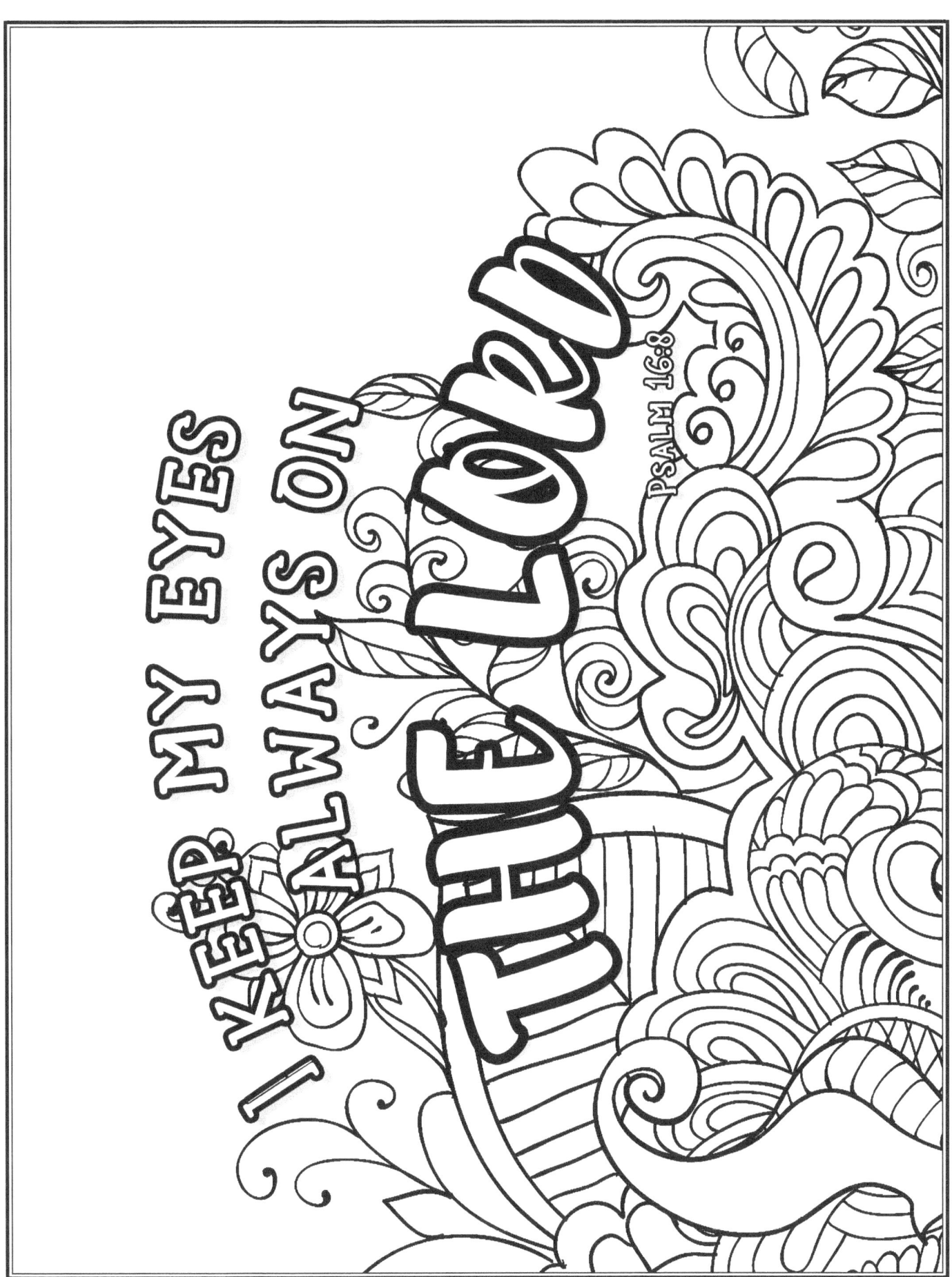

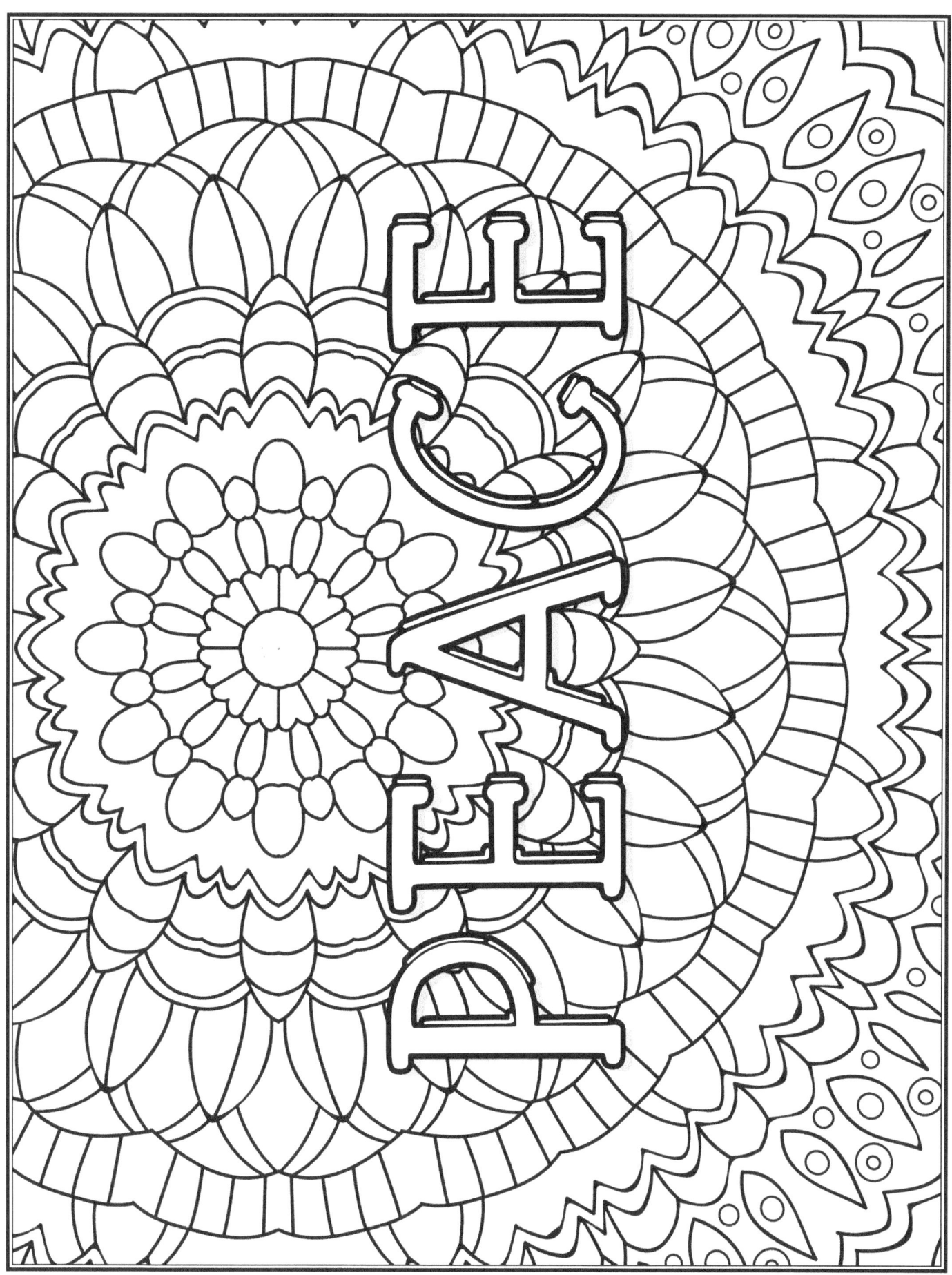

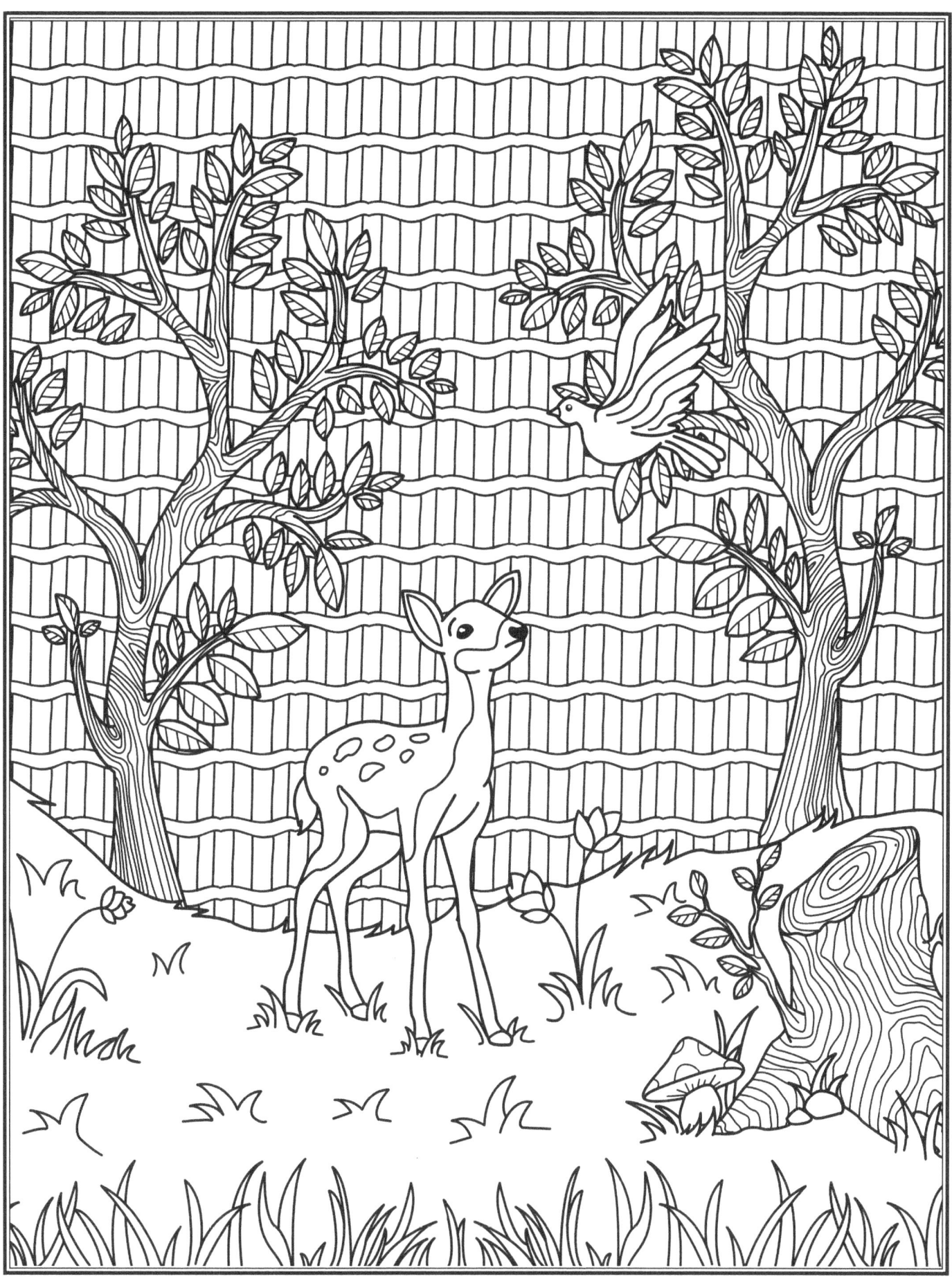

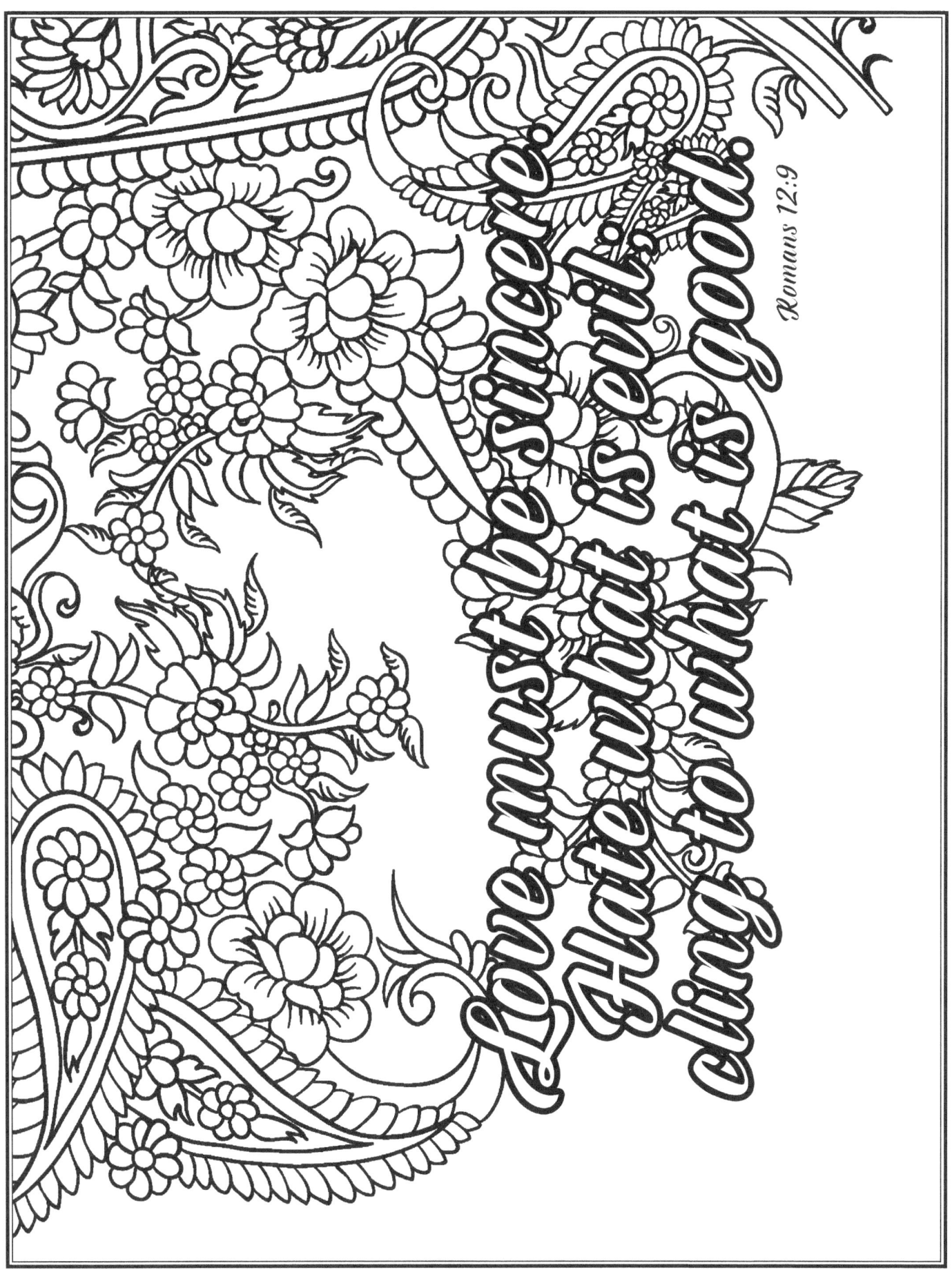

Love must be sincere. Hate what is evil; cling to what is good.

Romans 12:9

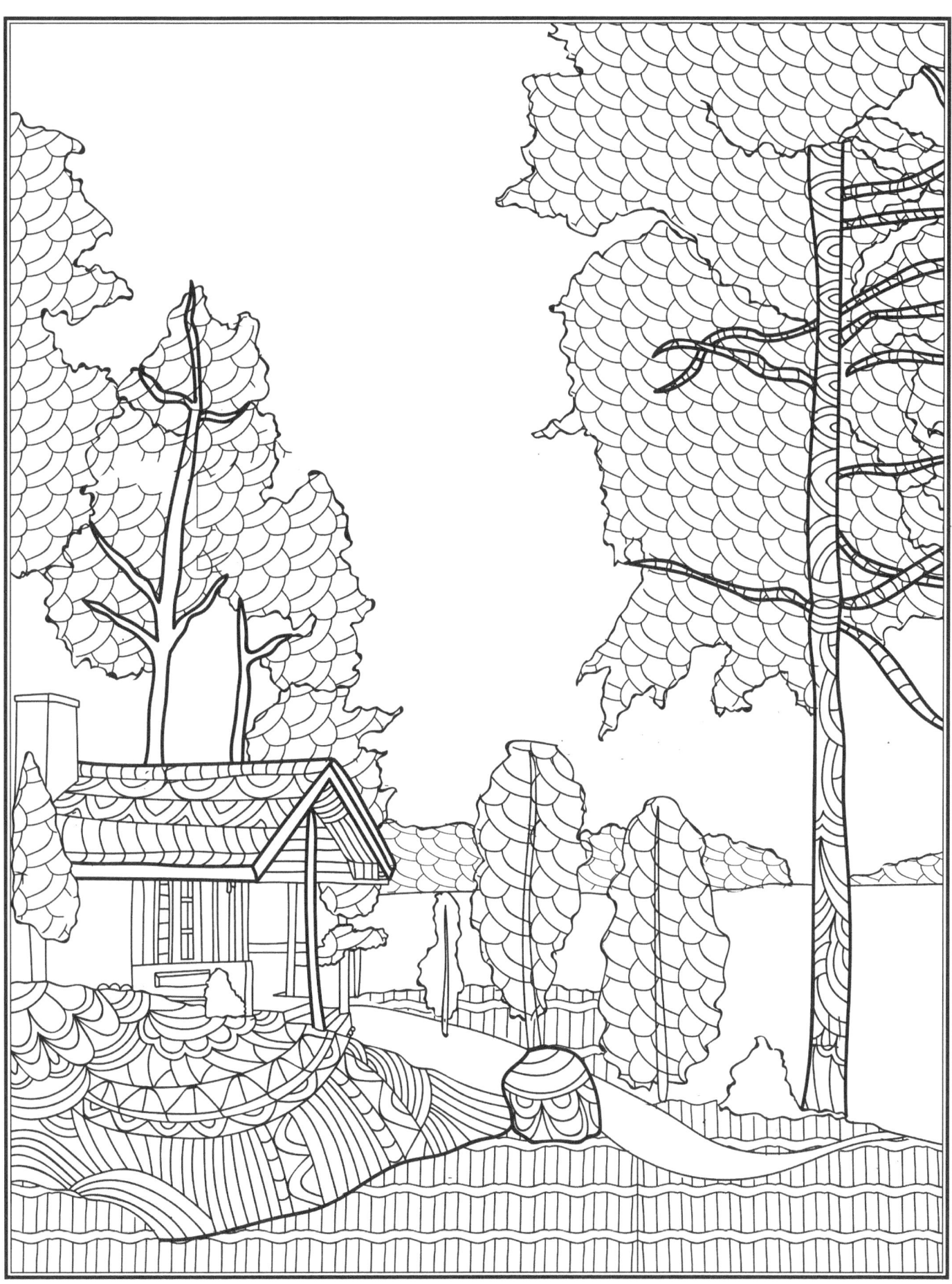

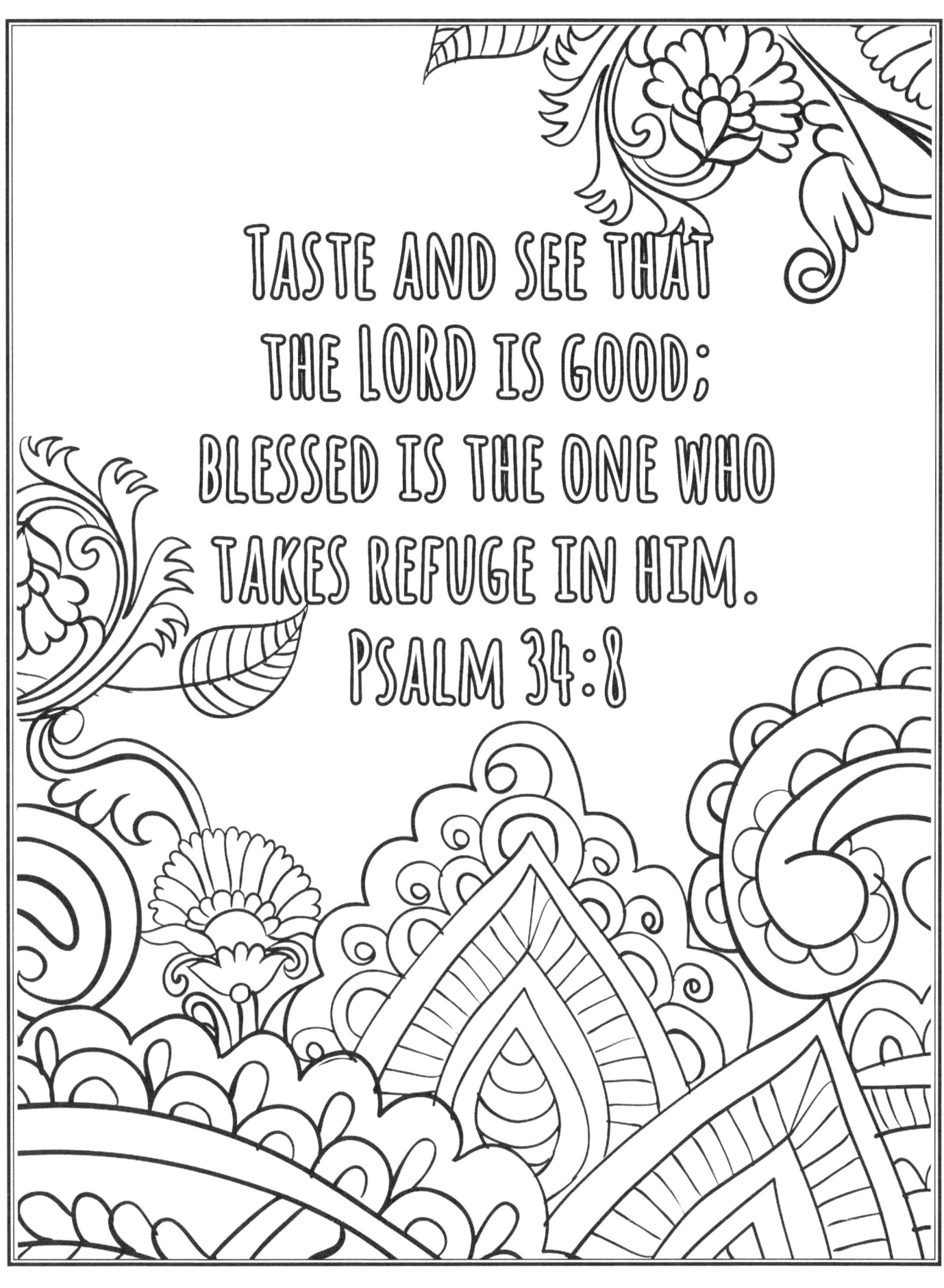

Taste and see that the LORD is good; blessed is the one who takes refuge in him. Psalm 34:8